From Persephone, With Love

The Companion to *Love Letters From Hades*

By Emily Brandt

ISBN: 9798223704423

First edition. September 21, 2023.

Written by Emily Brandt.

Cover designed by: Alyssa Verbert

For more information please email:
emilybrandt.writer@gmail.com

I wrote the last one for you.

This one is for me.

Introduction

When I wrote *Love Letters From Hades*, I knew that the story wasn't over; I had so much more to say, and the words seemed unending as they flowed out of me.

This time, I've written from Persephone's perspective. As we follow her over the course of a year, we see how different her journey is from Hades'. We also see how two lonely people can find solace and hope in one another.

No, this book is not myth-accurate, but that is the beauty of mythology. It changes and shapes itself as time goes on. In it, we find ourselves reflected in ways we need to bring explanation and hope to our present selves.

I hope that you find hope and recovery in these pages and that your voice feels heard. Even if it feels like you're screaming into an empty cavern.

SUMMER

Life

Like a tiny sparrow too young to leave its nest

Its wings never quite ready for the fall

And suddenly

It all comes crashing down

Like a wildfire burning the world to ash

To begin anew

They wish to box me in

Give me names I do not claim

I am not just one thing

I am all

I am infinite

I am Dread Persephone

And

I am Maiden of Spring

Cover my bruises in mud

Slick as the hours of the night

Bathe me in the minerals of earth

I want to live for a tomorrow

That I will miss

It's just like little girls to disobey their parents

I will not sit prim and proper with a napkin on my
lap

Give me grit and pain and danger

Or I will die searching for it

For I bring life but have never felt *alive*

Men fear powerful women

The way our lips curve

And do not ask permission to speak

With rough hands

Worn from battering walls

Nails filed like daggers

Fine, I say

Fear me they can

And never will I be controlled again

Would you sing if you were placed in a cage

High above where you felt safe?

To spit in the face of anger and hostility

From those you were born to trust?

Why then is there surprise in your eyes

At the silent bursts that swallow me

And shroud me in gray shadows I cannot shake

From a body cold and unfed

Even in a world that is full of beauty and life

I find myself searching for the underbelly

Of the world that once brought me joy

That now I can only see as wicked

Today I feel older than the ground I lay upon

The grass playing in between my fingers

Running along them like children on a Summer

day

Soft like a melody and rough as a promise

I wonder how long I can stay in this place

In a world so peaceful

While a storm rips inside me

Begging for more with its claws

I yearn for a life I've yet to live

Far beyond the meadows and rain

But can I leave a world that has loved me so

Or am I doomed to discontent

I want to unfurl myself in the morning sun

Open my petals to the breeze

Raise my face to

Her beauty

And

Finally accept

That I am only myself

And that is the one thing

They will never take away from me

The morning comes

Same as every day

I awaken

Feeling dewdrops

And the colors of the world

Pouring into me

Like a warm stiff breeze

That swarms like bees

And moves the world over me

I stand watching it all go by

Day by endless day

Wishing only for the onyx sky

To return once more

Flecked with its pinpoint map

Toward a home, I've yet to find

How many times must I break this heart before

It stops begging to beat anymore?

No matter how many stitches I undo

I find it sewn together

By fate's thread of iron and steel

Even though they wrote songs and poems for
Helen and
Praised for her beauty, unlike any the world had
seen
Even *she* was condemned to male's cruel eye
To be nothing more than a face that men fought a
Bloody battle for

Worried not for what she wanted or loved
Did she watch the sunrise, same as me?
I wonder what words she would speak
Were she more than a marble bust to be gawked
upon
Or if one had cared to write it down

Dirt under shortened fingernails

Sweat dripping from slicked hair

Freckles from sunkissed afternoons

A maiden, innocent and bare

Tear-stained gowns and ripped skirts

Bloodied bruises tender on elbows and knees

Teeth broken from clenched jaws

A woman who begs you to see

I am who I am

Not who you wish me to be

Anger and all the glory with it

A child still caged within me

Trust is a funny thing, Mother

I don't bite your hand as it feeds me
And you never let me leave your sight

Leashed like a dog kept in a porcelain cage
Sedated not to break the eggshell glass

But I have teeth, and I have claws

Heavy heart few can carry

Made to break and

Filled with grief

That poison

Of flowers that once were roses

Wilted to nothing but memories of

Ghosts faded in the background of

Discolored photos and smudged

Paintings left unfinished on the table

On the easel where the bristles of the

Brush have hardened to stone and left

Somewhere forgotten

The loveliest of the bunch

Dies in captivity

Under a watchful eye

Kept in a vase

With water too old

Withering petals cry

Am I but a bouquet?

Softer than a blink

Gone with a sigh

I never learned to bite my tongue

And so words press against my chest

Until I choke on them like swallowed rebuttals

And mistress manners meant for one

fair fairer than I

Clouds cover my vision

I cannot see the light

Where is the way out of darkness

When all there is, is night?

I hear the beckoning call of the crow

Ushering me forth through the twisted trail

The breeze quickens and chills the skin

Pricking at me and prodding me forward

Into the blackness, I step

Unknowing where your guiding hand reaches

I leap into discovery, fear a distant worry

The wind whispers my name

Persephone, it calls. *Come to me.*

The ground opens and swallows me whole

Welcoming me like a childhood friend

I embrace the shadows like a lover

It's familiar.

It's *you*.

AUTUMN

Maybe I didn't *ask* to be taken

But when you offered your hand

I jumped.

I am hiding

(Do you seek?)

Can you find me?

In this labyrinth

First I'm here

Then I'm there

One swift foot ahead

Just out of reach

I never stay for long

Attachment is cruel

But in these moments

Hand touching hand

(I am caught)

And you are sought

When you're still young and foolish, as most of us
are,
You believe the world is peaceful, like a spring
meadow.

That nothing in the world could touch you.
Rarely do we witness the flood until it reaches our
feet.

And by then, *it's far too late.*

How many stories must show a woman's fate

sealed by the taste of fruit?

26

Is it so impossible for man to imagine I chose this

for myself?

They tell the tale like a spider

Spinning their webs and stories

Of glories and other meaningless ideals

Brought to us from others whose names

I've forgotten now

Remember this:

We all end up below with Hades

From the smallest fruit fly

To the bravest of warriors

And each should know a love

Worthy only of a life they've lived

I see the way your hands shake
How the work weighs on you
Pulls at your skin and

Carves divots in your face
I wish there were more to say
More to do and think

To take away the pain
I see deep in your eyes
I cannot help one like you

When I myself am broken
Like a rusty tool bent
Unable to fulfill a job

I didn't know I had

My lost, lonely soldier

The weight of the world seems too heavy

For one such as you

Who has carried it so long

And never speaking a word

I am so sorry for the dark thoughts

That blind me to your love

I wish to love you in the way you deserve, but there
is no taming the creatures of my mind.

32

I never thought people could change

We are creatures of habit

But then I saw you smile

And the flowers that grew

From the seeds you'd sewn

If nature can shift

And thrive where it once was impossible

So can I.

Lay your demons to rest

Your head may lay in my garden

I will keep you company

And together we shall weed and pick

The worst parts of ourselves

And find life in dead soil

The silence of these expanding caverns

Never ceases to open

A feeling of wonderment

And abandonment

For this is a life I chose

Though none from above will approve

I search through the maze of Hades

Searching, always searching for you

A sip

Only a sip

To ease a thirst

That ran in my blood

You quenched my soul

And I will pay for it forever

WINTER

I cannot sleep with the howling winds of Winter

It chills me to the bone

And the guilt I feel is no consolation

To be with you alone.

Sunrise

The glorious moment before the

World awakens and

Bustles with life once more

Peace is easy to find

Amongst the trees

That whisper *Good Morning*

With each passing breeze

Sunset

The fragile fleeting moment while the

World quiets and stares

At the painting of the clouds

As the bird croons the love it sings

And flaps their wings towards

Another morning with its golden rings

Yellow like the morning sun

And your smile

The feeling of falling in love

Over and over again

No matter how many months

Of sooty fog linger in my soul

I find the yellow of the morning

And find you new like shy Crocus

Up from the coldest obscurity of yesterday

All I wanted was stability

A love to depend on

Someone to return to

Over and over again

Someone who *wanted* me to return

And I know that in the end, this all means nothing.

That the world will keep turning.

42

But to you,

I am something more.

 Someone worth saving.

And that makes me sad anyway.

The work is never done

But rest your hands in mine

Find the interlude that plays in my smile

Come to bed, love

And loosen your chains for a while

Let tomorrow be tomorrow

Tonight, I am yours.

For just awhile

This love is magic I cannot see

Or touch

Or hear

But it is with me nonetheless

In the silent glances

And the touch of your hand

Ignite my bones in your aching passion

Find me alive in this place of death

I wanted nothing more than to be yours

Give me those promised desires

And let your flames devour me whole

My world was *daggers*

> Before you dulled the knife
>
> That pierced my wounds
>
> With only a touch of your hand
>
> And a whisper of hope

My heart is yours, entirely.

My mind, however, is hardly my own.

Sadness does not draw my lips to a frown

It is more a muted melancholy shade

A blanket under which I hide

If you could feel the grass under your feet

Hear the trill of good morning

Smell the sweet scent of life

You too would find yourself caged here

Fading into the gray

Wishing to cleanse yourself of the reek of death

I wonder if the trees miss their leaves in winter

Ever patient and stoic

They stand rooted and tall

When their leaves return are they the same?

The same shades of green take hold

They feel the same under soft fingertips

But others have died before them

Taken into the ground and morphed

Familiar and yet a substitute for those gone

A cycle of repeated death and life

Like all things fragile and necessary

I wonder if I will be the same when Spring returns

Please

Don't let me fade into the background of your life

Let my laughter permeate the walls

Don't forget our shared moments here

Please

Never wonder if I would stay

I don't want to be a forgotten silhouette on the wall

Pieces of me scattered and shattered on the floor

Please

Grasp my hand and clutch my heart

 I wish to see the world again

But not at this expense

Please

On my darkest nights, you are my lighthouse
Guiding me to safety
Away from the heavy waves and currents that
Drag and pull me down

With you, I can breathe again
And find my way to the shore
One breath at a time

You may rule the dead, my Grief,

But I am still the Mistress of Decay.

52

I do not miss the rain

Or sun

The feeling of soil in my toes

Nor fresh running water

But the *breeze*, Hades

That delicate rush of air

That pulls me up

I want to drown myself in it

You're not the villain

No matter what they tell you

Their whispers so gutting

Their tales wild as the flowers above

What they do not see they cannot understand

But I see you

For all you are

And all you will become

I stop the world between the ticks of the clock

For just a moment

There is peace in the silence

Too large to be filled

You and I

Standing here together

In a moment of bliss and hushed murmurs

Of snowdrops and dew

Here in the quiet

I find us again

Just before the clock resumes

And the moment passes

Before I noticed it had started

The story of us will exist long after the floods
overtake the land and smooth the crevices of
man-made atrocities

And the sky turns bloody as it echoes a war song
When the ocean becomes slick and dark like oil
And the creatures vanish in search of new life

Even when there is no one to hear the words
Our song will reverberate through the leaves of the
trees

And the branches will chime a melody
That brings in the winter air once again

Dance with me as we lift our spirits up

Praising and cheering for a new year

A new life that begins once again

A turning 'round and 'round

Pouring ourselves into our glasses

Melting like ice onto each other's lips

My love,

The flames of your anger bite the air

Choking all life that deigns to face you

Quiet that rumbling hate in your heart

Allow the Spring to rush instead

And cool the embers of your flesh

Calloused hands

Blistered feet

Work is never done

Wedding bands

Hearts beat

You finally found the one

Flowers wilt

Bluest eyes

Away together, we run

We play these games, you and I. Cat and mouse. Hunter and prey. One *just* out of reach. The other, ready for the kill. I stalk you in the bushes. Wondering. Waiting.

Together long enough for just a taste of sweet respite. Too short for a lifetime. Before the hunt is on again.

How nice it would be to love one another without
the world depending on us.

I feel like my life is an open suitcase

Always ready to go

Never prepared to stay

Today here

Tomorrow there

How long until I can unpack my suitcase

And hang my clothes in your closet?

Until I can rest easy

In a bed that is my own?

The pastel glow of morning light

Dissolves the frost that covers my heart

In shame and longing

I see you again, in the sunrise beams

Aching for just a moment longer in the silence

Where it is only you and I

Until tomorrow

Your outer shell

Like bedrock

Coats every pore

I will chisel away

Every day

Until I find you

Again

It's time for me to go again

Staying would delay the inevitable

Back again to the world above

A place no longer my own

Forget me not while I am gone

And I will search for you

Waiting to return again

Hoping for peace in a chaotic world

SPRING

We find ourselves again in this unending cycle

Death and Rebirth

Spring and Winter

Always leaving too soon to unpack

I leave my shoes at the door

Both a perpetual night

And eternal burning morning

Peace is the moment where I find myself

Beneath the haunting willow tree

Looking up at the brightest sky I've ever seen

Feeling the soft tufts of grass between my fingers

So serene in that moment

Like you were there, all along

And if I try hard enough

It feels as if you are

April rains fill my soul

Even the sky cries

When I feel everything

And yet nothing at all

Each Spring I fear the flowers will refuse to bloom again. As if maybe this is the last time they will forgive me.

I wish that you could see
the beauty of it all
The way the colors bloom
and the summer leaves that shiver

The sun with its pink mornings
And nights of staying true
The bees that buzz *'hello'*
And the iris' shade of blue

Like your soul matches mine
Though far away we are
Touching my heart I find
You have left a scar

I whisper your name to the flowers in hopes they
bring the message to you.

72

That even when the sun shines and life begins
anew, it is you I wish I could share each moment
with.

For you deserve to see it most of all.

I find I miss you in the moments between breaths

And in the peaceful dew of the morning

While even the birds rest above us

Safely in their nests

I find I miss myself when I am alone

Surrounded by those who claim to know me

Wishing to be back with someone who does

Safely in my nest

The rain in the morning is a melody in my mind. Each drop, a note on the staff of nature's refrain. It comforts me to shelter in the overcast morning. To sit alone and find peace in the cacophony of splatters on the dampened grass.

 I find you in the mists. Your shadow follows me even now. I do not find you in the sunshine on a Summer day, but rather in the refreshing chorus of Spring's heavy rains.

The flowers speak to me

Words so sweet

Like love's first whisper

It tickles my thoughts

And caresses my doubts

Until I forget I am alone

Rose colored lenses and rose gold afternoons

Slept under a sun burning so bright

It blinded me to the love

That grew from a pit in my chest

Pink petals in my hand

Wrinkled like love letters

Read a million times before

Into the air they flutter

Soft like butterfly wings

Or dragonfly flapping

So close to the pond they fly

The water gasping as they touch

For only a moment

    Before being plunged into the benthic bottom

Spring waters and their
Swollen bellies of beds
Pregnant with the ideas of
Spring and her merriment
Waiting to overflow and enrich
The world once again

How giving, and fruitful
The unbounded love of one
Who gives such life
Over and over again

I wish to do as nature does
But it's in my nature to refuse

I would not wish for a war to be fought

For one such as I

Save your useless bloodshed for one

Impressed by vulgar passions

Instead, I would have you mourn my absence

Within the irises of the evening light

And spend your life ripping apart the heart

You swore you'd never lose

It seems these days all I do is bring death to what I
cherish most.

You seem so far now

As if a road was laid between us

I am afraid to cross it

For the rocks will pierce my feet

I am not so nimble or graceful

I trip over the words I dare not speak

You never know the capacity of love until

You're alone in your thoughts wondering

Why you let the moments slip through your fingers

Like an hourglass, I feel the sand trickle

I want to enjoy the moments here

To feel the warm breeze dance across my skin

But my mind wanders back to you once more

The longing glance in your endless purgatory

I look to the sky searching for you again

Wishing for a single moment below

Beneath the obsidian night beside you

Falling endlessly into the abyss

A moment in that fiery pit burning inside like

passion

My love for you is thorns

It rips away the skin

Leaving nothing but rose-colored stains

On an ivory gown

I am a fool for your love. Each time I see you, it begins anew. As if a heart had never broken, and our lips had never met.

These comings and goings

Our meetups and heartbreaks

They never end, do they?

Like magnets, you and I

Forever begging to touch

But pressed wrong

And forced apart

I fear my fate parallels Pandora's

Sent as a punishment to mankind

Blamed for all that is wrong with the world

A figure draped in misery and dread

A curse set upon us all to wreak havoc

But curious minds will be curious

And women will be women

Harbingers of love and hope

With death clutched between our knuckles

And on the day my grief was so heavy in my hands
It clung to the air like desperate hands
The earth heard me then as drops fell
And the sky

began

to

weep

Don't fall into the darkness, my love

Never let the night swarm the clusters

Of your mind like fragments of memories

Wait for the sun to rise

And find your way home to me

It is there

Death surrounds me

Even on the brightest summer day

It lurks in the shadows

And crawls at my feet

Black like midnight

Sad as a grave

It beckons me back

Leaving the world to perish

For my own guilty pleasure

Take me to your Castle of Dread

No matter the pain

I will come back

                              I'll always come back

Characters

PERSEPHONE- Goddess of Spring, Queen of the Underworld, wife to Hades. Daughter of Demeter and Zeus.

HADES- God of wealth, King of the Underworld, husband to Persephone.

DEMETER- Goddess of the Harvest and Fertility, Mother to Persephone.

PANDORA- The first woman, created by Zeus. She opened "Pandora's Jar" and released all evils into the world except for one- hope.

HELEN- Helen of Troy, the most beautiful woman in ancient Greece. When she was taken by Paris of Troy, it began the Trojan War.

About the Author

A storyteller at heart, Emily has been writing her entire life. From the stage to the page, sharing dreams and telling tales of adventure and love are her biggest passions. She graduated with a BFA in Musical Theatre from Millikin University and currently resides in Belgium.

Also by Emily

Love Letters From Hades

The companion to *From Persephone, With Love*, *Love Letters From Hades* is a collection of poems that follows Hades, King of the Underworld, through an entire year cycle. As the seasons change, we watch Hades deal with raw emotions through his "letters" to Persephone. From his grief and doubt in Spring to the rekindling of his love in Autumn, there are poems for each and every soul. In these pages, you'll find comfort during your darkest days and hope that tomorrow will be a little bit brighter.